SONGS OF INNOCENCE

AND

SONGS OF EXPERIENCE

WILLIAM BLAKE

Red Axe Books

ISBN: 978-0993218392

CONTENTS

SONGS OF INNOCENCE

SONGS OF EXPERIENCE

Introduction

William Blake may be too dangerous to give to young people. He's too subversive; too sexually provocative; too persuasive; too off his trolly. Blake can mess with your head. I still blame him for turning my predicted A grade at Eng. Lit. A level into a C, so obsessed by him did I become to the exclusion of other authors on the exam syllabus. Blake so connects with the emotional make-up of the hormonal adolescent the effect can be brain washing. His sexual philosophy became mine; his firebrand of revolutionary politics also mine. He was an addictive drug. Amazing then that he is still pushed on 15, 16, 17 and 18 year olds in such large doses.

Yet during the intervening years we have developed a love/hate relationship. My admiration for the way he can use simple words to create complex imagery remains undimmed, but I resent him in equal measure for leading me astray, a combination of my naivety and his.

His Dark Materials author Philip Pullman describes coming across Blake at 16 as like the "joyful immediacy of a flame leaping to meet a gas jet", and it is how I felt at the same age. We both even chose the same *Complete Writings* as a school prize!

Pullman says: "The experience is not like learning to appreciate something that we once found difficult...and decide that yes, on balance, it is full of interesting and admirable things. It's a more visceral, physical sensation than that, and it comes most powerfully when we're young. Something awakes that was asleep, doors open that were closed, lights come on in all the windows of a palace inside us, the existence of which we never suspected...if Blake could inspire the sort of hellish rapture celebrated and howled about by (Allen) Ginsberg, then he was the sort of poet I needed to read. Hellish rapture was exactly what I most wanted."

Too often Blake is lumped in with his Romantic near contemporaries – Wordsworth, Coleridge and Shelley. But he's not really one of them. The stuff of nature played out differently in Blake's imagination so, for instance, the sea does not represent freedom but oppressive tyranny and starlit skies which couples might associate with romance as they canoodle under them have a more sinister meaning for Blake. But although he was largely unknown in his day Blake has had an extraordinary influence on the late 20th Century and the beginning of the 21st.

Blake was born a Londoner in November 1757 and lived there almost all his life as a painter, poet, printmaker, visionary, luminary and mystic. He died penniless in 1827, breathing his last at six o'clock one August evening "like the sighing of a gentle breeze". He believed artists are born and not made, and that his genius was heaven-sent.

As he said himself: "Knowledge of ideal beauty is not to be acquired. It is born with us. Innate ideas are in every man born with him...Man brings all that he has or can have into the world with him, man is born like a garden ready planted and sown. This world is too poor to produce one seed...The man who never in his minds and thoughts travelled to heaven is no artist."

Blake saw God at the age of four, the Old Testament prophet Ezekiel soon after, and a tree full of angels in the unlikely setting of Peckham Rye, and never stopped having visions.

"I have very little of Mr Blake's company," complained his wife, Kate. "He is always in paradise." He thought about sex quite a bit, too, so he has a lot in common with teenagers.

But his sexual philosophy is not a promiscuous free-for-all, but the liberation of sex within a committed relationship which, in his case, was with his wife. And there is no evidence that Blake was ever unfaithful during 45 years of marriage. See what he means in this poem from *Songs of Experience*

> A flower was offered to me:
> Such a flower as May never bore.
> But I said I've a Pretty Rose-tree,
> And I passed the sweet flower o-er.
>
> Then I want to my Pretty Rose-tree:
> To tend her by day and by night.
> But my Rose turned away with jealousy:
> And her thorns were my only delight.

This is a poem about fidelity and lust of the heart. The flower on offer is a young woman prepared to sleep with him, and she's obviously a temptation – *such a flower as May never bore* – but he says: "Look, sweetie, I'd love to go to bed with you but the wife is at home – *the Pretty Rose-Tree* – so I'd better not but thanks all the same."

Blake is too smug about this, overly pleased with himself for his own self-control, self-sacrifice and self-denial. So pleased that he trots off home to tell his wife all about it. There may have been some shouting, even a spot of dish throwing, but the bottom line is that his wife will not let him anywhere near her – *But my Rose turned away with jealousy / And her thorns were my only delight* – and so that night he was consigned to the couch.

This morality tale has Blake (or the central character of his imagination if it was not he) turning his back on what was on offer only because he was a married man, not because he did not want what was being served up on a plate. That was why his wife was so angry. What he should have said to the woman hitting on him was: "Look, I love my wife and I'm really not interested."

Blake got many of his ideas from abroad, from the Swedish philosopher Emmanuel Swedenborg, the Swiss alchemist Paracelsus, and the German mystic, Jakob Boehme. "What Blake derived from such sources was one version of stock European radicalism," says literary critic John Carey. "It's ingredients included freedom from repression, faith in the redeeming power of sex, the reversal of normal moral standards, worship of passion and energy, hatred of reason, science and commerce...Blake's formulations of this creed sound marvellous, but quickly nosedive if you treat them as real ideas. 'Sooner murder an infant in its cradle than nurse unacted desires'. Might that not be the slogan of every rapist?"

It might. It also might be interpreted as a slogan for 'free love', which is the way it was seen in the 1960s by a generation enjoying the sexual liberation the contraceptive pill brought about. Blake himself is not entirely clear on the issue, and even at the end of his life he was still talking about Swedenborg's injunction to share wives 'in common'. Yet no credence can be attached to the suggestion by some biographers that Blake ever wanted to take a 'second wife' as a surrogate mother in his childless marriage. He may well have had sexual fantasies which found expression in his poetry, but at heart he does seem to have believed in monogamy.

This confusion should not put us off reading Blake, and he was able to recognise the faults in some of his own ideas himself. But obscurity runs through all his poems, with the exception of some of the earliest ones and a few of the *Songs of Innocence*. Blake never went to a proper school – Henry Par's drawing school which he attended was just that – so he didn't learn the mental disciplines of Latin and Greek. In later life he picked up both languages without difficulty. But that lack of formal education made his grammar weak, so the sense of many of the poems has to be worked out by their general content.

Symbolism is the key. So when Blake is talking about roses, nurses or tigers he is usually thinking about something else. Pre-sexual Christian innocence symbols would include children, sheep, wild birds, wild flowers, green fields, dawn, dew, spring, shepherds, valleys and hills. Unrestrained, revolutionary and righteously destructive energy symbols are words like lions, tigers, wolves, eagles, noon, summer, fire, forges, swords, spears, chariots. These trip over into sexual symbols from uninhibited ecstasy to selfish power over loved ones and jealousy like dreams, branches of trees, gold, silver, moonlight, nets, cages, fairies, bows and arrows. And roses.

These overlap into corruption symbols of hypocrisy and secrecy and feature many of the things to be found in towns – looms, curtains, houses, snakes, evening, silence, disease. And oppression symbols whether personal, parental, political or religious such as priests, mills, forests, mountains, seas, caves, clouds, thunder, frost, night, stars, winter, stone, iron. The problem with Blake is that when he combines his symbolism with an elaborate, self-constructed mythology the poetry becomes almost unintelligible, and after 1794 he has his own home-made private language. It means that Blake is at his best in his simpler poems, like *Songs of Innocence and of Experience*.

This does not mean Blake was incapable of recognised poetic forms. He had a fine ear for rhyme and rhythm. Most traditional English poetry is written in iambic pentameter, ten syllables of five poetic feet with the stress falling on the second syllable of each foot. The opening line of Rupert Brooke's most famous poem is an excellent example of iambic pentameter:

*If **I**| should **die**| think **on**|ly **this**| of **me**.*

The stresses fall on the words Brooke wants to emphasise; I, die, this, me. But Blake preferred trochaic meter, in which the stress comes on the first syllable of the foot. Iambic tends to be reflective; trochaic assertive.

Blake's Introduction to his *Songs of Innocence* in 1789 is in trochaic trimeter, lines of trochees in three feet, with an added stressed syllable at the end of each line which seems to just dangle there until you realise its importance.

Piping| **down** the| **val**leys| **wild**

Piping| **songs** of| **pleas**ant| **glee**

This is in your face stuff, hitting you hard with *piping down* and *piping songs,* but the words which most stand out in these lines are *wild* and *glee.* Blake draws our attention to their contrast by placing them at the end of the lines with a stress on them. *Valleys wild* - normal speech would have wild valleys but because you lose the stress you can see why that wouldn't have worked – conjures up a dangerous place where we would be wise to tread warily. But, in his innocence, the piper sees none of that as he skips about piping his songs of pleasant glee. The reader gets a sense of foreboding, that something uncomfortable is on its way, which of course it is in *Songs of Experience.*

In the last stanza of the Introduction it seems the word 'I' should be most important, but the metre dictates otherwise. Blake wants us to notice the additional things the piper gets up to which is why the stress falls on 'And' not 'I'. Here he is, surrounded by beautiful, fresh, clear water and what does he do? Stains it with ink, that's what.

And having polluted the water he writes his *happy songs every child may joy to hear.* We know now these happy songs are concealing something unpleasant:

And I| **made** a| **rur**al| **pen**

And I| stained the| water| clear

And I| wrote my| happy| songs

Every| child may| joy to| hear

There is no evidence that when *Songs of Innocence* were completed Blake was planning their antithesis as *Songs of Experience* in 1794, though the possibility must have been tucked away in his mind somewhere. But in the five years which separates the two works he becomes more preoccupied with the nature of good and evil, and increasingly aware of the insufferable conditions around him in the streets of London where twenty people died of starvation each week. And once written the Experience poems always accompanied the Innocence ones in a single volume.

Blake biographer Jack Lindsay says: "Each poem in *Songs of Experience* has a poem in *Songs of Innocence* to which it is related. At times the connection is close; at times there is little more than the title that links. The themes of Experience are lack of freedom and openness in love, enslavement (especially of children) by deceit or force, the tyrannies exerted by law, state, and church."

So *Infant Joy* in Innocence is matched by *Infant Sorrow* in Experience where there is no longer anything joyful about being born

My mother groaned! My father wept.
Into the dangerous world I leapt:
Helpless, naked, piping loud:
Like a fiend hid in a cloud.

Struggling in my fathers hands:
Striving against my swaddling bands:
Bound and weary I thought best
To sulk upon my mother's breast.

Songs of Innocence and of Experience was the only one of Blake's illustrated books which enjoyed any popularity at the time. Songs for children with a moral message were fashionable in his day, and the Innocence poems were written when Blake was running a print shop which subsequently went bust. So there is more than a suspicion of a commercial motive in producing them, even though he claimed to despise commerce. As a journeyman engraver he even illustrated serials in *Ladies' Magazine*. But one wonders what parents who bought the book must have made of their purchase once they got it home. Blake may have been on the receiving end of some angry complaints.

Some of the symbolism is made obvious by our familiarity with it in other contexts; the lamb is a universal symbol of innocence and meekness just as the fox is one for cunning and the dove for peace. But in many of the *Songs of Innocence and of Experience* less obvious symbolism only becomes apparent by its repetition. Once we are conscious that each noun can mean something else the sense of what Blake is getting at can be grasped.

So the tiger is on one level a symbol of creative energy, but it is also just a tiger. Which allows Blake to question whether a god who made the gentle lamb can also be responsible for the raging violence of this beast. It is a theme he constantly returns to; why does God create terror? Which widens into the theological question the Church has never been quite able to adequately answer: if God is good why is there evil in the world? In the ending of *The Tyger* Blake does not directly answer this question either though we must assume he knew it to be a yes – God makes everything; lamb and tiger; good and evil

> When the stars threw down their spears,
> And water'd heaven with their tears,
> Did he smile his work to see?
> Did he who made the lamb make thee?

It's as if Blake is shouting at heaven: "Oi, you up there, mate. What are you all about then?" So in Blake's *Proverbs of Hell* "prisons are built with the stones of law, brothels with bricks of religion." And "the pride of the peacock is the glory of God, the lust of the goat is the bounty of God, the wrath of the lion is the wisdom of God" and "the nakedness of woman is the work of God".

It is the oppressiveness of Church and state which leads to prisons and brothels; sex is not evil but the repression of it is; a woman without her clothes arouses a man and that is how God intended it. A friend was shocked to come across Blake and Kate in their small summer house one afternoon reciting passages from *Paradise Lost* both naked. They had undressed for the occasion to better get into character. "Come in," said Blake."It's only Adam and Eve, you know!"

The symbolism is not static like a code in which the same word can be deciphered each time to reveal its meaning, just as a lion does not always represent royalty but can also symbolise pride. Blake's genius lay in the versatility of his symbolism, and to turn it into a dictionary you can just look up is to do that genius a disservice. And if it was that simple the poems would be lifeless.

As with all the greatest poetry the best way to understand Blake is to read and re-read, to let the words wash over and seep inside you, until you can *feel* their meaning. And that feeling will vary with each individual reader; your interpretation is as good as mine. We know that valleys, hills and pastures mean freedom and joy, and that thunder is the wrath of God. But in Blake's mind that thunder may have symbolised a kind of deified George III; in ours it will translate into something completely different, unfamiliar as we are with living under the rule of the bonkers pre-Regency king.

As Blake explained: "I assert for myself that I do not behold the outward creation, and that to me it is hindrance and not action... 'What!' it will be questioned, 'when the sun rises do you not see a round disc of fire somewhat like a guinea?' 'Oh no, no; I see an innumerable company of the heavenly host crying, 'Holy, holy, holy, is the Lord God Almighty.' "

In *Songs of Innocence*

> The sun does arise
> And make happy the skies.

But in *Songs of Experience*

> The sun arises in the east
> Clothed in robes of blood and gold.

For Blake there were three stages of human development – innocence, experience and grace. The child is innocent, incapable of evil, or comprehending it, so intrinsically good. It is why adolescents and adults blush and young children do not. We become aware of our sinful nature, and are shamed by it. The older you are the less likely your face is to redden. This is the state of grace, understanding sin and putting it into perspective. You are basically good because you have won the battle against evil.

For Blake desires are good and we should not restrain them, nor be fettered by rules or laws or by the state or by morality. Sex is nothing to be ashamed of and it is God's will we are sexual beings and all that entails – so enjoy uninhibited sexual pleasure within a committed relationship. Love and wisdom are infinite and cannot be measured. Don't be held back; let it all hang out; go for it; do what turns you on. As Blake said: "Damn braces, bless relaxes."

Along with sexual liberation Blake believed passionately in political freedom as well, a surefire winner with rebellious youngsters. The age he lived in was a time of huge political turmoil he was bound to be affected by what with the American Revolution of 1775 and the French Revolution of 1789. It would be a while before the terror which followed the upheavals in France would become apparent and Blake approved of ordinary people taking control of their own destinies, of those who had formerly been subjects becoming citizens. Though none of this should overly concern us in *Songs of Innocence and of Experience*.

Blake was the master of the aphorism. There are the straightforward ones..."what is now proved was once only imagined..."truth can never be told so as to be understood, and not to be believed"..."as the air to a bird or the sea to a fish, so is contempt to the contemptible"..."you never know what is enough unless you know what is more than enough"..."can that be love that drinks another like the sponge drinks water"..."no bird soars too high if he soars with his own wings". There are the problematic ones..."those who restrain their desire, do so because theirs is weak enough to be restrained"..."he who desires but acts not breeds pestilence".

And the ones which urge us to grab life with exuberance and not hold back..."expect poison from the standing water"..."the cistern contains, the fountain overflows." But what are we to make of "one law for the lion and ox is oppression" when the law should apply equally to everyone?

Much of what Blake came to believe was influenced by his own marriage to Catherine Boucher. They were both in their early twenties when they met and it was love at first sight. She was a pretty young woman with large, dark brown eyes. He first saw her at her parents' house in Battersea having just been dumped by a girlfriend. Catherine was sympathetic at which, according to a contemporary source, Blake said: "Do you pity me?" She replied: "Yes, indeed I do." "Then I love you," said Blake. The couple knew immediately they were made for each other, which led to Blake's belief that a man and a woman are two halves waiting to come together to make one whole.

On the whole I believed that, too. That perfect love happened when two people became one; that you are just half a person until you find your soul mate who is the other half and the two halves are united. I now know that not to be selfless love but love addiction leading to control and manipulation of a partner and ultimately to a doomed relationship. Love only lasts when two people are free individuals who choose to come together and stay together. In that way they are not two dependent halves of the same whole, but two independent wholes whose sense of being does not rely on being validated by the other. And this is where, I think, Blake led me astray. What he was describing is co-dependency.

Co-dependency is like the baby's relationship with its mother. Until he is about six months old the baby sees his mother as an extension of himself, their two circles overlapping until the baby begins to realise he is his own circle and his mother her own circle. The baby becomes all one. We have a word for it: alone.

Co-dependency is the need to be needed, which is why for the love addict rejection is so painful. Just as the relationship is obsessive because there seems no self-worth without it, so the end of it is all-consuming, too, confirming to the addict he or she really is worthless after all. And until that cycle is broken, the co-dependent will be condemned to live in one tortured hell after another. The idea of people as two halves destined to make one whole circle between them was not a Blake original; it had been around since antiquity. But it was through Blake I first encountered it, and such was its appeal the notion persisted with me for years.

Was the relationship between Blake and Kate a co-dependent one? At 200 years remove it would be folly to attempt a psychological judgement. At the beginning of their marriage she was illiterate or nearly so, and signed the wedding register with an X. It was Blake who taught her to read and write. And she seems a little too ready to embrace his weird ideas which she would later articulate vehemently herself.

So it is possible she was overawed by his intellect. For his part Blake was content to let Kate mother him. So the seeds of co-dependency are there, though it is impossible to know how, or if, they grew. Their union seems to be have been one of the most successful in literary history, so it would be presumptuous to dismiss it as emotionally unhealthy. Let's leave it there.

Blake's poems work on a number of levels, and as a hymn *Jerusalem* must be his best known. It has been misunderstood as an attack on the Satanic mills of the Industrial Revolution, but it is even more subversive than that. As Blake scholar Stanley Gardner says, it is a condemnation of what Blake saw as the un-Christian god worshipped in churches; a god of repression feeding one man under the whip of another; a god who pitted man against man; a god who denied with iron law the joys of the imagination and the senses. *Jerusalem,* written as a preface to *Milton's A Poem* and set to music during the First World War, is packed with Blake's oppression symbols:

> And did those feet in ancient time
> Walk upon England's mountains green?
> And was the holy Lamb of God
> On England's pleasant pastures seen?
> And did the Countenance Divine
> Shine forth upon our clouded hills?
> And was Jerusalem builded here
> Among these dark Satanic mills?

Bring me my bow of burning gold:
Bring me my arrows of desire:
Bring me my spear: O clouds unfold!
Bring me my chariot of fire.
I will not cease from mental fight,
Nor shall my sword sleep in my hand
Till we have built Jerusalem
In England's green and pleasant land.

It is the churches of his day which are the *"mills of Satan"*, and his revolt against them is symbolised in the *"bow of burning gold"*, the *"arrows of desire"*, the *"chariot of fire"*. The poem implies the rebuilding of a city in which poverty, oppression and disease are no more, a rebirth based on spiritual regeneration, *till we have built Jerusalem in England's green and pleasant land.*

Gardner explains the symbolism of open pastures and enclosed spaces: "It is the difference between free, uninhibited joy and sophisticated pleasure. The symbol of the garden fostered with care, walled and fenced, belongs not to Innocence but Experience. There are no gardens in the *Songs of Innocence*." Let's look at two of the allegories Blake planted in his garden, the sick rose and the sunflower.

O Rose thou art sick.
The Invisible worm,
That flies in the night
In the howling storm:

Has found out thy bed
Of crimson joy:
And his dark secret love
Does thy life destroy.

On one level this is simply a rose being eaten by an insect. On another it might be about a sexually transmitted disease; *crimson joy* is a highly sexualised image. But peel away these layers and deeper down is the message that *secret love* is the worst sort and no good can come of it. Love should be open and celebrated and committed, so this appears to be an attack on adultery, or shameful promiscuity. Yet when we cross the flower bed in *Songs of Experience* to meet the sunflower we're being told to do what we want to do, not to dither because we might miss out, no restraining our desires

> Ah, Sun-flower, weary of time,
> Who countest the steps of the Sun,
> Seeking after that sweet golden clime
> Where the traveller's journey is done:
>
> Where the Youth pined away with desire,
> And the pale Virgin shrouded in snow
> Arise from their graves, and aspire
> Where my Sun-flower wishes to go.

The sunflower, the youth and the virgin are of one in this poem; full of longing, yearning for what they cannot attain. The sunflower is rooted in the earth, living out its days turning its head towards a sun it can never reach, while the youth and virgin who might be expected to get it on together can only 'arise' and 'aspire' in the same fruitless way. In *Songs of Innocence* desire finds fulfilment; in *Songs of Experience* it remains unfulfilled.

This theme continues as we move to the orchard

> I asked a thief to steal me a peach:
> He turned up his eyes.
> I asked a lithe lady to lie her down:
> Holy and meek she cries.
>
> As soon as I went
> An angel came.
> He winked at the thief
> And smiled at the dame.
>
> And without one word said
> Had a peach from the tree
> And still as a maid

Enjoyed the lady.

In this next poem Blake imagines himself as a virgin dreaming of love and once more he is raging against nursing unacted desires. The maiden is petted and fondled by an angel and she encourages his attention by simulating grief to gain sympathy. She desperately wants to take this further but nevertheless refuses to let him make love to her and so off he goes.

When they meet again it is too late

> I dreamt a Dream! What can it mean?
> And that I was a maiden Queen:
> Guarded by an Angel mild:
> Witless woe, was ne'er beguiled!
>
> And I wept both night and day
> And he wiped my tears away
> And I wept both day and night
> And hid from him my heart's delight.
>
> So he took his wings and fled:
> Then the moon blushed rosy red:
> I dried my tears and armed my fears,
> With ten thousand shields and spears.
>
> Soon my Angel came again:
> I was armed he came in vain:
> For the time of youth was fled
> And grey hairs were on my head.

There are clear contradictions in Blake's writing, and that may be what T.S. Eliot was getting at when he said Blake's poems have the unpleasantness of great poetry... "a peculiar honesty which, in a world too frightened to be honest, is peculiarly terrifying." As life itself is full of contradictions, never clear cut, not one thing or the other, perhaps Blake's honesty is art imitating life.

In answer to my opening remarks, of course young people

should consume Blake's poetry, and do so with relish. If they are to learn the skills necessary to challenge controversial ideas then they must first be confronted by them. Their minds need to float freely, not be wrapped in cotton wool because that leads to woolly thinking. And those right-on politically correct fascists who would ban certain speakers from their university campuses because they might say something offensive would do well to remember that. All I am urging on Blake readers of any age is to maintain a healthy scepticism, to have their wits and critical faculties about them, to keep a wary eye on the emotional response. Beware anything which initially blows your mind away. Then, having armed the intellect with "ten thousand shields and spears", lay back and enjoy some of the most wonderful English literature ever written.

Nigel Nelson

INTRODUCTION

Piping down the valleys wild,
   Piping songs of pleasant glee,
On a cloud I saw a child,
   And he laughing said to me:

'Pipe a song about a Lamb!'
   So I piped with merry cheer.
'Piper, pipe that song again.'
   So I piped: he wept to hear.

'Drop thy pipe, thy happy pipe;
   Sing thy songs of happy cheer!'
So I sung the same again,
   While he wept with joy to hear.

'Piper, sit thee down and write
   In a book, that all may read.'
So he vanished from my sight;
   And I plucked a hollow reed,

And I made a rural pen,
   And I stained the water clear,
And I wrote my happy songs
   Every child may joy to hear.

THE SHEPHERD

How sweet is the shepherd's sweet lot!
From the morn to the evening he strays;
He shall follow his sheep all the day,
And his tongue shall be fillèd with praise.

For he hears the lambs' innocent call,
And he hears the ewes' tender reply;
He is watchful while they are in peace,
For they know when their shepherd is nigh.

THE ECHOING GREEN

The sun does arise,
And make happy the skies;
The merry bells ring
To welcome the Spring;
The skylark and thrush,
The birds of the bush,
Sing louder around
To the bells' cheerful sound;
While our sports shall be seen
On the echoing green.

Old John, with white hair,
Does laugh away care,
Sitting under the oak,
Among the old folk.
They laugh at our play,
And soon they all say,
'Such, such were the joys
When we all—girls and boys—
In our youth-time were seen
On the echoing green.'

Till the little ones, weary,
No more can be merry:
The sun does descend,
And our sports have an end.
Round the laps of their mothers
Many sisters and brothers,
Like birds in their nest,
Are ready for rest,
And sport no more seen
On the darkening green.

THE LAMB

Little lamb, who made thee?
Does thou know who made thee,
Gave thee life, and bid thee feed
By the stream and o'er the mead;
Gave thee clothing of delight,
Softest clothing, woolly, bright;
Gave thee such a tender voice,
Making all the vales rejoice?
Little lamb, who made thee?
Does thou know who made thee?

Little lamb, I'll tell thee;
Little lamb, I'll tell thee:
He is callèd by thy name,
For He calls Himself a Lamb.
He is meek, and He is mild,
He became a little child.
I a child, and thou a lamb,
We are callèd by His name.
Little lamb, God bless thee!
Little lamb, God bless thee!

THE LITTLE BLACK BOY

My mother bore me in the southern wild,
  And I am black, but O my soul is white!
White as an angel is the English child,
  But I am black, as if bereaved of light.

My mother taught me underneath a tree,
  And, sitting down before the heat of day,
She took me on her lap and kissèd me,
  And, pointing to the East, began to say:

'Look on the rising sun: there God does live,
  And gives His light, and gives His heat away,
And flowers and trees and beasts and men receive
  Comfort in morning, joy in the noonday.

'And we are put on earth a little space,
  That we may learn to bear the beams of love;
And these black bodies and this sunburnt face
  Are but a cloud, and like a shady grove.

'For, when our souls have learned the heat to bear,
  The cloud will vanish, we shall hear His voice,
Saying, "Come out from the grove, my love and care,
  And round my golden tent like lambs rejoice."'

Thus did my mother say, and kissed me,
  And thus I say to little English boy.
When I from black, and he from white cloud free,
  And round the tent of God like lambs we joy,

I'll shade him from the heat till he can bear
  To lean in joy upon our Father's knee;
And then I'll stand and stroke his silver hair,
  And be like him, and he will then love me.

THE BLOSSOM

Merry, merry sparrow!
Under leaves so green
A happy blossom
Sees you, swift as arrow,
Seek your cradle narrow,
Near my bosom.
Pretty, pretty robin!
Under leaves so green
A happy blossom
Hears you sobbing, sobbing,
Pretty, pretty robin,
Near my bosom.

THE CHIMNEY-SWEEPER

When my mother died I was very young,
And my father sold me while yet my tongue
Could scarcely cry 'Weep! weep! weep! weep!'
So your chimneys I sweep, and in soot I sleep.

There's little Tom Dacre, who cried when his head,
That curled like a lamb's back, was shaved; so I said,
'Hush, Tom! never mind it, for, when your head's bare,
You know that the soot cannot spoil your white hair.'

And so he was quiet, and that very night,
As Tom was a-sleeping, he had such a sight!—
That thousands of sweepers, Dick, Joe, Ned, and Jack,
Were all of them locked up in coffins of black.

And by came an angel, who had a bright key,
And he opened the coffins, and set them all free;
Then down a green plain, leaping, laughing, they run
And wash in a river, and shine in the sun.

Then naked and white, all their bags left behind,
They rise upon clouds, and sport in the wind:
And the angel told Tom, if he'd be a good boy,
He'd have God for his father, and never want joy.

And so Tom awoke, and we rose in the dark,
And got with our bags and our brushes to work.
Though the morning was cold, Tom was happy and warm:
So, if all do their duty, they need not fear harm.

THE LITTLE BOY LOST

'Father, father, where are you going?
　O do not walk so fast!
　Speak, father, speak to your little boy,
Or else I shall be lost.'

The night was dark, no father was there,
　The child was wet with dew;
The mire was deep, and the child did weep,
　And away the vapour flew.

THE LITTLE BOY FOUND

The little boy lost in the lonely fen,
  Led by the wandering light,
  Began to cry, but God, ever nigh,
Appeared like his father, in white.

He kissed the child, and by the hand led,
  And to his mother brought,
Who in sorrow pale, through the lonely dale,
  Her little boy weeping sought.

LAUGHING SONG

When the green woods laugh with the voice of joy,
And the dimpling stream runs laughing by;
When the air does laugh with our merry wit,
And the green hill laughs with the noise of it;

When the meadows laugh with lively green,
And the grasshopper laughs in the merry scene;
When Mary and Susan and Emily
With their sweet round mouths sing 'Ha ha he!'

When the painted birds laugh in the shade,
Where our table with cherries and nuts is spread:
Come live, and be merry, and join with me,
To sing the sweet chorus of 'Ha ha he!'

A CRADLE SONG

Sweet dreams, form a shade
O'er my lovely infant's head!
Sweet dreams of pleasant streams
By happy, silent, moony beams!

Sweet Sleep, with soft down
Weave thy brows an infant crown!
Sweet Sleep, angel mild,
Hover o'er my happy child!

Sweet smiles, in the night
Hover over my delight!
Sweet smiles, mother's smiles,
All the livelong night beguiles.

Sweet moans, dovelike sighs,
Chase not slumber from thy eyes!
Sweet moans, sweeter smiles,
All the dovelike moans beguiles.

Sleep, sleep, happy child!
All creation slept and smiled.
Sleep, sleep, happy sleep,
While o'er thee thy mother weep.

Sweet babe, in thy face
Holy image I can trace;
Sweet babe, once like thee
Thy Maker lay, and wept for me:

Wept for me, for thee, for all,
When He was an infant small.
Thou His image ever see,
Heavenly face that smiles on thee!

Smiles on thee, on me, on all,
Who became an infant small;
Infant smiles are His own smiles;
Heaven and earth to peace beguiles.

THE DIVINE IMAGE

To Mercy, Pity, Peace, and Love,
   All pray in their distress,
   And to these virtues of delight
Return their thankfulness.

For Mercy, Pity, Peace, and Love,
   Is God our Father dear;
And Mercy, Pity, Peace, and Love,
   Is man, His child and care.

For Mercy has a human heart;
   Pity, a human face;
And Love, the human form divine:
   And Peace the human dress.

Then every man, of every clime,
   That prays in his distress,
Prays to the human form divine:
   Love, Mercy, Pity, Peace.

And all must love the human form,
   In heathen, Turk, or Jew.
Where Mercy, Love, and Pity dwell,
   There God is dwelling too.

HOLY THURSDAY

'Twas on a holy Thursday, their innocent faces clean,
The children walking two and two, in red, and blue, and green:
Grey-headed beadles walked before, with wands as white as snow,
Till into the high dome of Paul's they like Thames waters flow.

O what a multitude they seemed, these flowers of London town!
Seated in companies they sit, with radiance all their own.
The hum of multitudes was there, but multitudes of lambs,
Thousands of little boys and girls raising their innocent hands.

Now like a mighty wind they raise to heaven the voice of song,
Or like harmonious thunderings the seats of heaven among:
Beneath them sit the aged men, wise guardians of the poor.
Then cherish pity, lest you drive an angel from your door.

NIGHT

The sun descending in the West,
The evening star does shine;
The birds are silent in their nest,
And I must seek for mine.
   The moon, like a flower
   In heaven's high bower,
   With silent delight,
   Sits and smiles on the night.

Farewell, green fields and happy groves,
Where flocks have took delight,
Where lambs have nibbled, silent moves
The feet of angels bright;
   Unseen, they pour blessing,
   And joy without ceasing,
   On each bud and blossom,
   And each sleeping bosom.

They look in every thoughtless nest
Where birds are covered warm;
They visit caves of every beast,
To keep them all from harm:
   If they see any weeping
   That should have been sleeping,
   They pour sleep on their head,
   And sit down by their bed.

When wolves and tigers howl for prey,
They pitying stand and weep;
Seeking to drive their thirst away,
And keep them from the sheep.
   But, if they rush dreadful,
   The angels, most heedful,
   Receive each mild spirit,
   New worlds to inherit.

And there the lion's ruddy eyes
Shall flow with tears of gold:

And pitying the tender cries,
And walking round the fold:
    Saying: 'Wrath by His meekness,
    And, by His health, sickness,
    Is driven away
    From our immortal day.

'And now beside thee, bleating lamb,
I can lie down and sleep,
Or think on Him who bore thy name,
Graze after thee, and weep.
    For, washed in life's river,
    My bright mane for ever
    Shall shine like the gold,
    As I guard o'er the fold.'

SPRING

Sound the flute!
Now it's mute!
Birds delight,
Day and night,
Nightingale,
In the dale,
Lark in sky,—
Merrily,
Merrily, merrily to welcome in the year.

Little boy,
Full of joy;
Little girl,
Sweet and small;
Cock does crow,
So do you;
Merry voice,
Infant noise;
Merrily, merrily to welcome in the year.

Little lamb,
Here I am;
Come and lick
My white neck;
Let me pull
Your soft wool;
Let me kiss
Your soft face;
Merrily, merrily we welcome in the year.

NURSE'S SONG

When voices of children are heard on the green,
  And laughing is heard on the hill,
My heart is at rest within my breast,
  And everything else is still.
'Then come home, my children, the sun is gone down,
  And the dews of night arise;
Come, come, leave off play, and let us away,
  Till the morning appears in the skies.'

'No, no, let us play, for it is yet day,
  And we cannot go to sleep;
Besides, in the sky the little birds fly,
  And the hills are all covered with sheep.'
'Well, well, go and play till the light fades away,
  And then go home to bed.'
The little ones leaped, and shouted, and laughed,
  And all the hills echoèd.

INFANT JOY

'I have no name;
I am but two days old.'
What shall I call thee?
'I happy am,
Joy is my name.'
Sweet joy befall thee!

Pretty joy!
Sweet joy, but two days old.
Sweet joy I call thee:
Thou dost smile,
I sing the while;
Sweet joy befall thee!

A DREAM

Once a dream did weave a shade
O'er my angel-guarded bed,
That an emmet lost its way
Where on grass methought I lay.

Troubled, wildered, and forlorn,
Dark, benighted, travel-worn,
Over many a tangled spray,
All heart-broke, I heard her say:

'O my children! do they cry,
Do they hear their father sigh?
Now they look abroad to see,
Now return and weep for me.'

Pitying, I dropped a tear:
But I saw a glow-worm near,
Who replied, 'What wailing wight
Calls the watchman of the night?'

'I am set to light the ground,
While the beetle goes his round:
Follow now the beetle's hum;
Little wanderer, hie thee home!'

ON ANOTHER'S SORROW

Can I see another's woe,
And not be in sorrow too?
Can I see another's grief,
And not seek for kind relief?

Can I see a falling tear,
And not feel my sorrow's share?
Can a father see his child
Weep, nor be with sorrow filled?

Can a mother sit and hear
An infant groan, an infant fear?
No, no! never can it be!
Never, never can it be!

And can He who smiles on all
Hear the wren with sorrows small,
Hear the small bird's grief and care,
Hear the woes that infants bear—

And not sit beside the nest,
Pouring pity in their breast,
And not sit the cradle near,
Weeping tear on infant's tear?

And not sit both night and day,
Wiping all our tears away?
O no! never can it be!
Never, never can it be!

He doth give His joy to all:
He becomes an infant small,
He becomes a man of woe,
He doth feel the sorrow too.

Think not thou canst sigh a sigh,
And thy Maker is not by:
Think not thou canst weep a tear,
And thy Maker is not near.

O He gives to us His joy,
That our grief He may destroy:
Till our grief is fled and gone
He doth sit by us and moan.

INTRODUCTION

Hear the voice of the Bard,
Who present, past, and future, sees;
Whose ears have heard
The Holy Word
That walked among the ancient trees;

Calling the lapséd soul,
And weeping in the evening dew;
That might control
The starry pole,
And fallen, fallen light renew!

'O Earth, O Earth, return!
Arise from out the dewy grass!
Night is worn,
And the morn
Rises from the slumbrous mass.

p. 34'Turn away no more;
Why wilt thou turn away?
The starry floor,
The watery shore,
Is given thee till the break of day.'

EARTH'S ANSWER

Earth raised up her head
From the darkness dread and drear,
Her light fled,
Stony, dread,
And her locks covered with grey despair.

'Prisoned on watery shore,
Starry jealousy does keep my den
Cold and hoar;
Weeping o'er,
I hear the father of the ancient men.

'Selfish father of men!
Cruel, jealous, selfish fear!
Can delight,
Chained in night,
The virgins of youth and morning bear.

'Does spring hide its joy,
When buds and blossoms grow?
Does the sower
Sow by night,
Or the ploughman in darkness plough?

'Break this heavy chain,
That does freeze my bones around!
Selfish, vain,
Eternal bane,
That free love with bondage bound.'

THE CLOD AND THE PEBBLE

'Love seeketh not itself to please,
  Nor for itself hath any care,
But for another gives its ease,
  And builds a heaven in hell's despair.'

So sung a little clod of clay,
  Trodden with the cattle's feet,
But a pebble of the brook
  Warbled out these metres meet:

'Love seeketh only Self to please,
  To bind another to its delight,
Joys in another's loss of ease,
  And builds a hell in heaven's despite.'

HOLY THURSDAY

Is this a holy thing to see
  In a rich and fruitful land,—
Babes reduced to misery,
  Fed with cold and usurous hand?

Is that trembling cry a song?
  Can it be a song of joy?
And so many children poor?
  It is a land of poverty!

And their sun does never shine,
  And their fields are bleak and bare,
And their ways are filled with thorns,
  It is eternal winter there.

For where'er the sun does shine,
  And where'er the rain does fall,
Babe can never hunger there,
  Nor poverty the mind appal.

THE LITTLE GIRL LOST

In futurity
I prophesy
That the earth from sleep
(Grave the sentence deep)

Shall arise, and seek
For her Maker meek;
And the desert wild
Become a garden mild.

In the southern clime,
Where the summer's prime
Never fades away,
Lovely Lyca lay.

Seven summers old
Lovely Lyca told.
She had wandered long,
Hearing wild birds' song.

'Sweet sleep, come to me,
Underneath this tree;
Do father, mother, weep?
Where can Lyca sleep?

'Lost in desert wild
Is your little child.
How can Lyca sleep
If her mother weep?

'If her heart does ache,
Then let Lyca wake;
If my mother sleep,
Lyca shall not weep.

'Frowning, frowning night,
O'er this desert bright
Let thy moon arise,
While I close my eyes.'

Sleeping Lyca lay,
While the beasts of prey,
Come from caverns deep,
Viewed the maid asleep.

The kingly lion stood,
And the virgin viewed:
Then he gambolled round
O'er the hallowed ground.

Leopards, tigers, play
Round her as she lay;
While the lion old
Bowed his mane of gold,

And her bosom lick,
And upon her neck,
From his eyes of flame,
Ruby tears there came;

While the lioness
Loosed her slender dress,
And naked they conveyed
To caves the sleeping maid.

THE LITTLE GIRL FOUND

All the night in woe
Lyca's parents go
Over valleys deep,
While the deserts weep.

Tired and woe-begone,
Hoarse with making moan,
Arm in arm, seven days
They traced the desert ways.

Seven nights they sleep
Among shadows deep,
And dream they see their child
Starved in desert wild.

Pale through pathless ways
The fancied image strays,
Famished, weeping, weak,
With hollow piteous shriek.

Rising from unrest,
The trembling woman pressed
With feet of weary woe;
She could no further go.

In his arms he bore
Her, armed with sorrow sore;
Till before their way
A couching lion lay.

Turning back was vain:
Soon his heavy mane
Bore them to the ground,
Then he stalked around,

Smelling to his prey;
But their fears allay
When he licks their hands,
And silent by them stands.

They look upon his eyes,
Filled with deep surprise;
And wondering behold
A spirit armed in gold.

On his head a crown,
On his shoulders down
Flowed his golden hair.
Gone was all their care.

'Follow me,' he said;
'Weep not for the maid;
In my palace deep,
Lyca lies asleep.'

Then they followèd
Where the vision led,
And saw their sleeping child
Among tigers wild.

To this day they dwell
In a lonely dell,
Nor fear the wolvish howl
Nor the lion's growl.

THE CHIMNEY-SWEEPER

A little black thing among the snow,
Crying! 'weep! weep!' in notes of woe!
'Where are thy father and mother? Say!'—
'They are both gone up to the church to pray.

'Because I was happy upon the heath,
And smiled among the winter's snow,
They clothed me in the clothes of death,
And taught me to sing the notes of woe.

'And because I am happy and dance and sing,
They think they have done me no injury,
And are gone to praise God and His priest and king,
Who made up a heaven of our misery.'

NURSE'S SONG

When the voices of children are heard on the green,
   And whisperings are in the dale,
The days of my youth rise fresh in my mind,
   My face turns green and pale.

Then come home, my children, the sun is gone down,
   And the dews of night arise;
Your spring and your day are wasted in play,
   And your winter and night in disguise.

THE SICK ROSE

O rose, thou art sick!
  The invisible worm,
That flies in the night,
  In the howling storm,

Has found out thy bed
  Of crimson joy,
And his dark secret love
  Does thy life destroy.

THE FLY

Little Fly,
Thy summer's play
My thoughtless hand
Has brushed away.

Am not I
A fly like thee?
Or art not thou
A man like me?

For I dance,
And drink, and sing,
Till some blind hand
Shall brush my wing.

If thought is life
And strength and breath,
And the want
Of thought is death;

Then am I
A happy fly.
If I live,
Or if I die.

THE ANGEL

I dreamt a dream! What can it mean?
And that I was a maiden Queen
Guarded by an Angel mild:
Witless woe was ne'er beguiled!

And I wept both night and day,
And he wiped my tears away;
And I wept both day and night,
And hid from him my heart's delight.

So he took his wings, and fled;
Then the morn blushed rosy red.
I dried my tears, and armed my fears
With ten thousand shields and spears.

Soon my Angel came again;
I was armed, he came in vain;
For the time of youth was fled,
And grey hairs were on my head.

THE TYGER

Tyger, tyger, burning bright
In the forests of the night,
What immortal hand or eye
Could frame thy fearful symmetry?

In what distant deeps or skies
Burnt the fire of thine eyes?
On what wings dare he aspire?
What the hand dare seize the fire?

And what shoulder and what art
Could twist the sinews of thy heart?
And, when thy heart began to beat,
What dread hand and what dread feet?

What the hammer? what the chain?
In what furnace was thy brain?
What the anvil? what dread grasp
Dare its deadly terrors clasp?

When the stars threw down their spears,
And watered heaven with their tears,
Did He smile His work to see?
Did He who made the lamb make thee?

Tyger, tyger, burning bright
In the forests of the night,
What immortal hand or eye
Dare frame thy fearful symmetry?

MY PRETTY ROSE TREE

A flower was offered to me,
  Such a flower as May never bore;
But I said, 'I've a pretty rose tree,'
  And I passed the sweet flower o'er.

Then I went to my pretty rose tree,
  To tend her by day and by night;
But my rose turned away with jealousy,
  And her thorns were my only delight.

AH, SUNFLOWER

Ah, sunflower, weary of time,
  Who countest the steps of the sun;
Seeking after that sweet golden clime
  Where the traveller's journey is done;

Where the Youth pined away with desire,
  And the pale virgin shrouded in snow,
Arise from their graves, and aspire
  Where my Sunflower wishes to go!

THE LILY

The modest Rose puts forth a thorn,
The humble sheep a threat'ning horn:
While the Lily white shall in love delight,
Nor a thorn nor a threat stain her beauty bright.

THE GARDEN OF LOVE

I went to the Garden of Love,
  And saw what I never had seen;
A Chapel was built in the midst,
  Where I used to play on the green.

And the gates of this Chapel were shut,
  And 'Thou shalt not' writ over the door;
So I turned to the Garden of Love
  That so many sweet flowers bore.

And I saw it was filled with graves,
  And tombstones where flowers should be;
And priests in black gowns were walking their rounds,
  And binding with briars my joys and desires.

THE LITTLE VAGABOND

Dear mother, dear mother, the Church is cold;
But the Alehouse is healthy, and pleasant, and warm.
Besides, I can tell where I am used well;
Such usage in heaven will never do well.

But, if at the Church they would give us some ale,
And a pleasant fire our souls to regale,
We'd sing and we'd pray all the livelong day,
Nor ever once wish from the Church to stray.

Then the Parson might preach, and drink, and sing,
And we'd be as happy as birds in the spring;
And modest Dame Lurch, who is always at church,
Would not have bandy children, nor fasting, nor birch.

And God, like a father, rejoicing to see
His children as pleasant and happy as He,
Would have no more quarrel with the Devil or the barrel,
But kiss him, and give him both drink and apparel.

LONDON

I wander through each chartered street,
   Near where the chartered Thames does flow,
A mark in every face I meet,
   Marks of weakness, marks of woe.

In every cry of every man,
   In every infant's cry of fear,
In every voice, in every ban,
   The mind-forged manacles I hear:

How the chimney-sweeper's cry
   Every blackening church appals,
And the hapless soldier's sigh
   Runs in blood down palace-walls.

But most, through midnight streets I hear
   How the youthful harlot's curse
Blasts the new-born infant's tear,
   And blights with plagues the marriage hearse.

THE HUMAN ABSTRACT

Pity would be no more
If we did not make somebody poor,
And Mercy no more could be
If all were as happy as we.

And mutual fear brings Peace,
Till the selfish loves increase;
Then Cruelty knits a snare,
And spreads his baits with care.

He sits down with holy fears,
And waters the ground with tears;
Then Humility takes its root
Underneath his foot.

Soon spreads the dismal shade
Of Mystery over his head,
And the caterpillar and fly
Feed on the Mystery.

And it bears the fruit of Deceit,
Ruddy and sweet to eat,
And the raven his nest has made
In its thickest shade.

The gods of the earth and sea
Sought through nature to find this tree,
But their search was all in vain:
There grows one in the human Brain.

INFANT SORROW

My mother groaned, my father wept:
Into the dangerous world I leapt,
Helpless, naked, piping loud,
Like a fiend hid in a cloud.

Struggling in my father's hands,
Striving against my swaddling bands,
Bound and weary, I thought best
To sulk upon my mother's breast.

A POISON TREE

I was angry with my friend:
I told my wrath, my wrath did end.
I was angry with my foe:
I told it not, my wrath did grow.

And I watered it in fears
Night and morning with my tears,
And I sunnèd it with smiles
And with soft deceitful wiles.

And it grew both day and night,
Till it bore an apple bright,
And my foe beheld it shine,
And he knew that it was mine,—

And into my garden stole
When the night had veiled the pole;
In the morning, glad, I see
My foe outstretched beneath the tree.

A LITTLE BOY LOST

'Nought loves another as itself,
  Nor venerates another so,
Nor is it possible to thought
  A greater than itself to know.

'And, father, how can I love you
  Or any of my brothers more?
I love you like the little bird
  That picks up crumbs around the door.'

The Priest sat by and heard the child;
  In trembling zeal he seized his hair,
He led him by his little coat,
  And all admired his priestly care.

And standing on the altar high,
  'Lo, what a fiend is here!' said he:
'One who sets reason up for judge
  Of our most holy mystery.'

The weeping child could not be heard,
  The weeping parents wept in vain:
They stripped him to his little shirt,
  And bound him in an iron chain,

And burned him in a holy place
  Where many had been burned before;
The weeping parents wept in vain.
  Are such things done on Albion's shore?

A LITTLE GIRL LOST

Children of the future age,
Reading this indignant page,
Know that in a former time
Love, sweet love, was thought a crime.

In the age of gold,
Free from winter's cold,
Youth and maiden bright,
To the holy light,
Naked in the sunny beams delight.

Once a youthful pair,
Filled with softest care,
Met in garden bright
Where the holy light
Had just removed the curtains of the night.

There, in rising day,
On the grass they play;
Parents were afar,
Strangers came not near,
And the maiden soon forgot her fear.

Tired with kisses sweet,
They agree to meet
When the silent sleep
Waves o'er heaven's deep,
And the weary tired wanderers weep.

To her father white
Came the maiden bright;
But his loving look,
Like the holy book,
All her tender limbs with terror shook.

Ona, pale and weak,
To thy father speak!
O the trembling fear!

O the dismal care
That shakes the blossoms of my hoary hair!'

A DIVINE IMAGE

Cruelty has a human heart,
  And Jealousy a human face;
Terror the human form divine,
  And Secrecy the human dress.

The human dress is forgèd iron,
  The human form a fiery forge,
The human face a furnace sealed,
  The human heart its hungry gorge.

A CRADLE SONG

Sleep, sleep, beauty bright,
Dreaming in the joys of night;
Sleep, sleep; in thy sleep
Little sorrows sit and weep.

Sweet babe, in thy face
Soft desires I can trace,
Secret joys and secret smiles,
Little pretty infant wiles.

As thy softest limbs I feel,
Smiles as of the morning steal
O'er thy cheek, and o'er thy breast
Where thy little heart doth rest.

O the cunning wiles that creep
In thy little heart asleep!
When thy little heart doth wake,
Then the dreadful light shall break.

THE SCHOOLBOY

I love to rise in a summer morn,
  When the birds sing on every tree;
The distant huntsman winds his horn,
  And the skylark sings with me:
  O what sweet company!

But to go to school in a summer morn,—
  O it drives all joy away!
Under a cruel eye outworn,
  The little ones spend the day
  In sighing and dismay.

Ah then at times I drooping sit,
  And spend many an anxious hour;
Nor in my book can I take delight,
  Nor sit in learning's bower,
  Worn through with the dreary shower.

How can the bird that is born for joy
  Sit in a cage and sing?
How can a child, when fears annoy,
  But droop his tender wing,
  And forget his youthful spring!

O father and mother if buds are nipped,
  And blossoms blown away;
And if the tender plants are stripped
  Of their joy in the springing day,
  By sorrow and care's dismay,—

How shall the summer arise in joy,
  Or the summer fruits appear?
Or how shall we gather what griefs destroy,
  Or bless the mellowing year,
  When the blasts of winter appear?

TO TIRZAH

Whate'er is born of mortal birth
Must be consumèd with the earth,
To rise from generation free:
Then what have I to do with thee?

The sexes sprung from shame and pride,
Blowed in the morn, in evening died;
But mercy changed death into sleep;
The sexes rose to work and weep.

Thou, mother of my mortal part,
With cruelty didst mould my heart,
And with false self-deceiving tears
Didst blind my nostrils, eyes, and ears,

Didst close my tongue in senseless clay,
And me to mortal life betray.
The death of Jesus set me free:
Then what have I to do with thee?

THE VOICE OF THE ANCIENT BARD

Youth of delight! come hither
And see the opening morn,
Image of Truth new-born.
Doubt is fled, and clouds of reason,
Dark disputes and artful teazing.
Folly is an endless maze;
Tangled roots perplex her ways;
How many have fallen there!
They stumble all night over bones of the dead;
And feel—they know not what but care;
And wish to lead others, when they should be led.

Printed in Great Britain
by Amazon.co.uk, Ltd.,
Marston Gate.